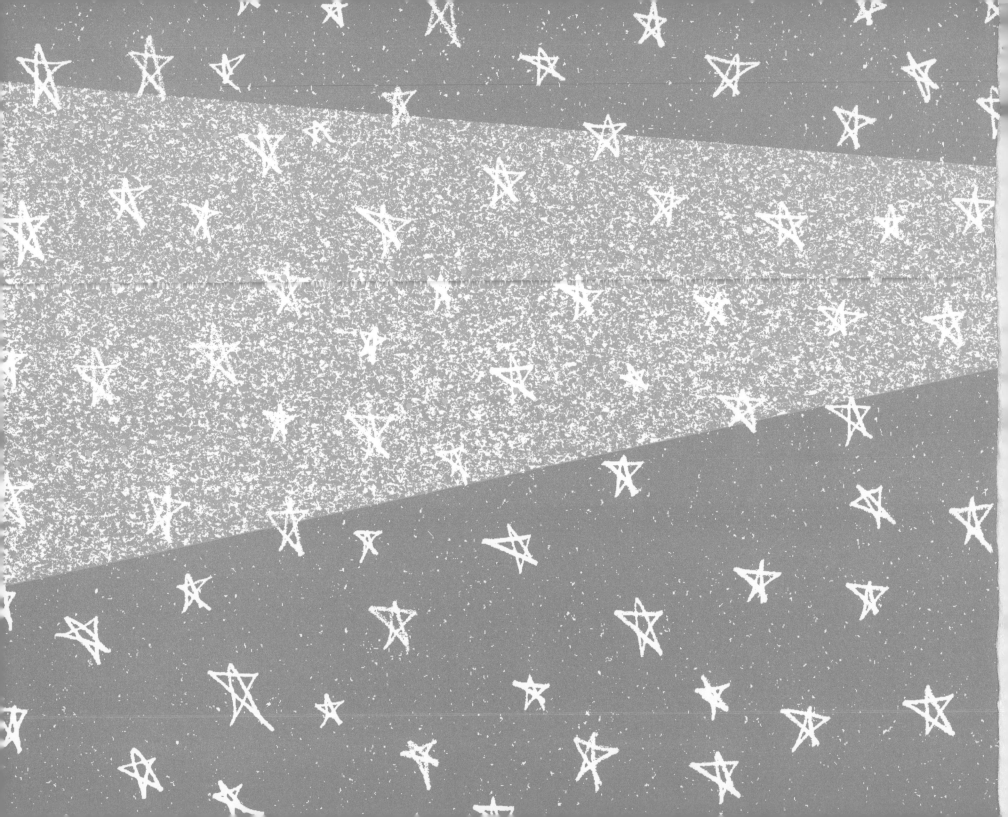

Older Than the Stars

Karen C. Fox • Illustrated by Nancy Davis

Charlesbridge

For my shining stars, Steve and Ben
—K. C. F.

For Mike, Brien, and Cameron: you are my wish upon a star
—N. D.

Special thanks to R. Hank Donnelly, astrophysicist at the Center for Naval Analyses

Published by Charlesbridge
85 Main Street
Watertown, MA 02472
(617) 926-0329
www.charlesbridge.com

Library of Congress Cataloging-in-Publication Data
Fox, Karen C.
    Older than the stars / Karen C. Fox ; illustrated by Nancy Davis.
       p. cm.
    ISBN 978-1-57091-787-5 (reinforced for library use)
1. Cosmology—Juvenile literature. 2. Big Bang theory—Juvenile literature.
3. Atoms—Juvenile literature. I. Davis, Nancy, ill. II. Title.
QB983.F69 2010
523.1—dc22   2009004304

Printed in China
(hc) 10 9 8 7 6 5 4 3 2 1

Illustrations done with pencil, cut paper, and potato and eraser prints,
    then digitally composed
Hand lettering by Nancy Davis
Text type set in Billy
Color separations by Chroma Graphics, Singapore
Printed and bound September 2009 by Jade Productions
    in Heyuan, Guangdong, China
Production supervision by Brian G. Walker
Designed by Diane M. Earley and Nancy Davis

You are older than the dinosaurs.

Older than the earth.

Older than the sun and all the planets.

You are older than the stars.

You are as old as the universe itself.

This is the

Billions of years ago, the universe popped into existence. It was smaller than a speck of dust, but so heavy no one could have picked it up. Suddenly, BANG!— the tiny universe swelled up like the fastest growing bubble ever. It grew millions of times bigger in the blink of an eye.

when the world began.

These are

The universe grew and grew. As it grew, tiny bits called protons, neutrons, and electrons formed. The bits whizzed here and there, back and forth, around and around like a bunch of bees.

The BiTs

that were born in the bang
when the world began.

These are the blocks

that formed from the bits ►

that were born in the bang

when the world began. ◄

The bits zigged this way and zagged that way, and sometimes they bumped into each other. When this happened they stuck together and formed something called atoms. Almost everything in the world is made of atoms. They are the building blocks of the universe. The first atoms were helium and hydrogen, two very light gases.

This is the gas

that spun from the blocks

that formed from the bits

Soon the universe was a jumble of helium and hydrogen atoms. Over millions of years, gravity pulled the atoms together until they grew into enormous clouds that were the size of galaxies, or even bigger.

in a giant puff

that were born in the bang   when the world began.

This is the star of red-hot stuff

that burst from the gas in a giant puff

that spun from the blocks

that formed from the bits

that were born in the bang

when the world began.

Inside each giant cloud, gravity pulled the atoms together. It got more and more crowded. When two atoms crashed into each other, they melted together, or fused, in a burst of light and heat. The cloud became a blazing star.

These are the atoms so strong and tough

in a giant puff   that spun from the blocks   that formed from that formed in the star of red-hot stuff   that burst from the gas

In the heart of the star, the atoms kept crowding into each other. Every time two smaller atoms fused together, they formed a bigger atom. Helium and hydrogen melted together to form medium-sized atoms like oxygen and carbon.

the bits   that were born in the bang   when the world began.

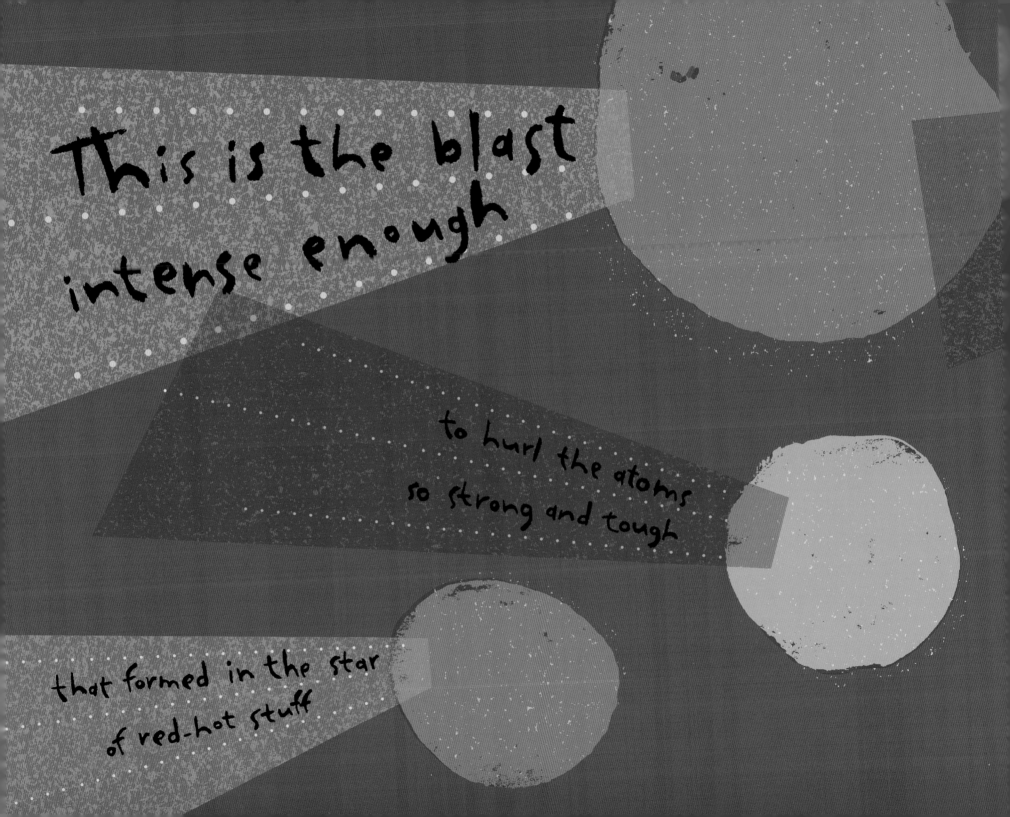

This is the blast
intense enough

to hurl the atoms
so strong and tough

that formed in the star
of red-hot stuff

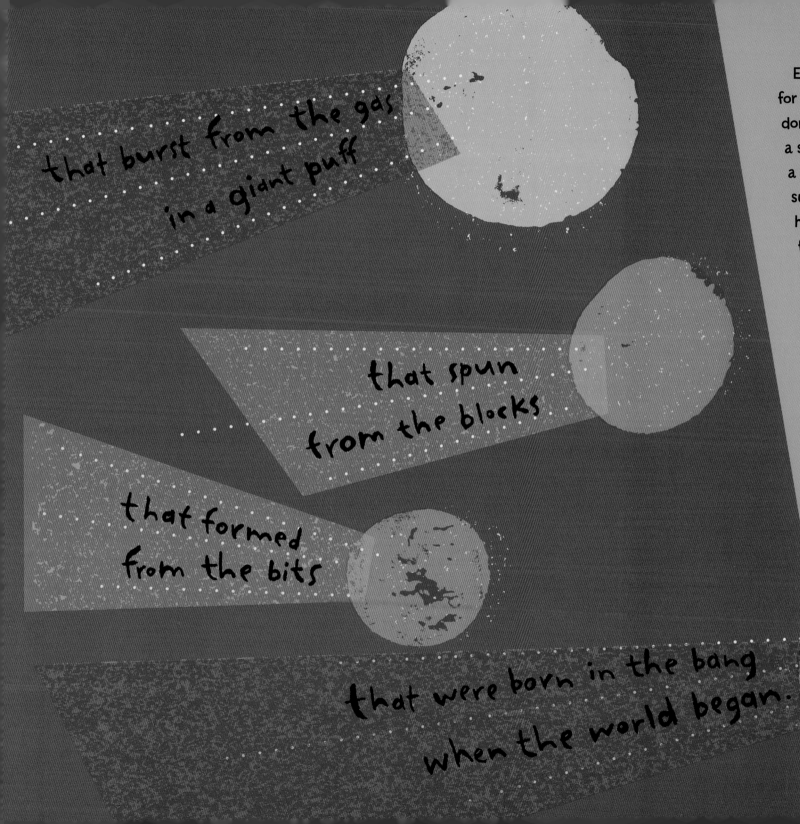

that burst from the gas
in a giant puff

that spun
from the blocks

that formed
from the bits

that were born in the bang
when the world began.

Each star shone brightly for billions of years. But stars don't live forever. Whenever a star died, it exploded in a giant fireball called a supernova. The searing heat of the supernova forced some of the star's atoms to melt together into new metals like iron, copper, and gold. The explosion sent all the atoms—big and small—hurtling through the universe in all directions.

The scattered atoms collected into new clouds of gas, which formed new stars.

Every time a new star was born, it kept right on making atoms.

Every time a new star grew old and died, it exploded and flung its atoms into space.

This is the dust, so old and new,

thrown from the blast intense enough

to hurl the atoms so strong and tough

that formed in the star of red-hot stuff

that burst from the gas in a giant puff

that spun from the blocks

that formed from the bits

that were born in the bang

when the world began.

This is the sun, our daily view,

Five billion years ago, right where our solar system is today, a cloud of atoms formed. As the cloud spun around and around, it flattened out like a giant plate.

At the center of the cloud, atoms fused together, creating light and heat. The center grew hotter and hotter until it turned into a star. That star is our sun.

The rest of the stuff in the spinning cloud began to stick together in dusty clumps. Each clump grew bigger and bigger until it turned into a planet.

When the world began,

in the bang

that were born

from the bits

that formed

that spun from the blocks

gas in a giant puff

that was born from

that burst from the

the dust, so old and new,

star of red-hot stuff

thrown from the blast

intense enough

to hurl the atoms

so strong and tough

that formed in the

This is the planet green and blue

that circles the sun, our daily view,

that was born from the dust, so old and new,

thrown from the blast intense enough

to hurl the atoms so strong and tough

that formed in the star of red-hot stuff

that burst from the gas in a giant puff

that spun from the blocks

that formed from the bits

that were born in the bang

when the world began.

The earth formed 4.5 billion years ago out of all sorts of atoms made by the stars. There was oxygen, hydrogen, lead, gold, and more. At first the young earth was a boiling hot soup of all these ingredients. But as the soup cooled, it separated into land and oceans.

In time, some of the atoms
in the ocean joined together
to form tiny living creatures.
At first these creatures were
so simple they didn't think
or even swim—they just
floated in the water.
But over time they
evolved, getting bigger
and more complex.
Life on Earth
had begun.

These are the plants and animals, too,

our daily view, that was born from the dust, so old and new,

strong and tough that formed in the star of red-hot stuff

the blocks that formed from the bits that were born in the bang

that grow on the planet green and blue   that circles the sun.

thrown from the blast intense enough   to hurl the atoms so

that burst from the gas in a giant puff   that spun from

when the world began.

Over billions of years the first small life-forms evolved into countless types of plants and animals. The living things depended on the atoms around them. Plants needed atoms in the water, air, and soil. Animals received oxygen from the air and other atoms, like iron, from their food. When a new animal was born, it was made from all those same atoms. And when it died, its atoms were released back into the ground.

These are the people just like you

who live with the plants and animals, too,

that grow on the planet green and blue

that circles the sun, our daily view,

that was born from the dust, so old and new,

thrown from the blast intense enough

to hurl the atoms so strong and tough

that formed in the star of red-hot stuff

that burst from the gas in a giant puff

that spun from the blocks

that formed from the bits

that were born in the bang

when the world began.

About 600,000 years ago, humans appeared. They absorbed atoms whenever they breathed, drank, or ate.

Those humans had children, and their children had children. You are one of those children, descended from the first humans— all made from the same atoms that the earth was.

The iron in your blood may have once been part of molten lava from a volcano. The carbon in your fingernails may have been part of a tree leaf. And the oxygen in your lungs was probably once breathed by dinosaurs.

You are older than the earth.

But before any of these atoms
helped create the earth, they formed
in stars long ago and far away. You are
made from atoms that were made in stars
that were made from tiny particles that
were created when the universe began.

Older than the sun and all the planets.

Older than the stars.

You are as old as the universe itself.

Time Line of the Universe

0 seconds
The universe, tinier than a speck of dust, pops into existence. It is billions of times hotter than our sun.

first fraction of a second
The entire universe expands dramatically in the blink of an eye.

first second
The universe cools to below 18 billion °F (10 billion °C), and neutrons, protons, and electrons begin to form. All the protons, neutrons, and electrons around today were made in the Big Bang when the universe was only a second old.

first 3 minutes
The universe keeps cooling. Protons, neutrons, and electrons begin to stick together. The centers of the first atoms form.

300,000 years
The universe expands enough for light to flow freely across space. The light allows the universe to be seen for the first time. Most of the helium and hydrogen atoms in the universe today were created by this time. (This includes all the helium used to blow up floating balloons.)

1–3 million years
Helium and hydrogen atoms clump together into clouds of gas that will become stars.

100 million years
The first stars begin to shine. In the hearts of stars, even bigger atoms form. Every time a star dies and explodes, even more atoms form and are spread out across the universe.

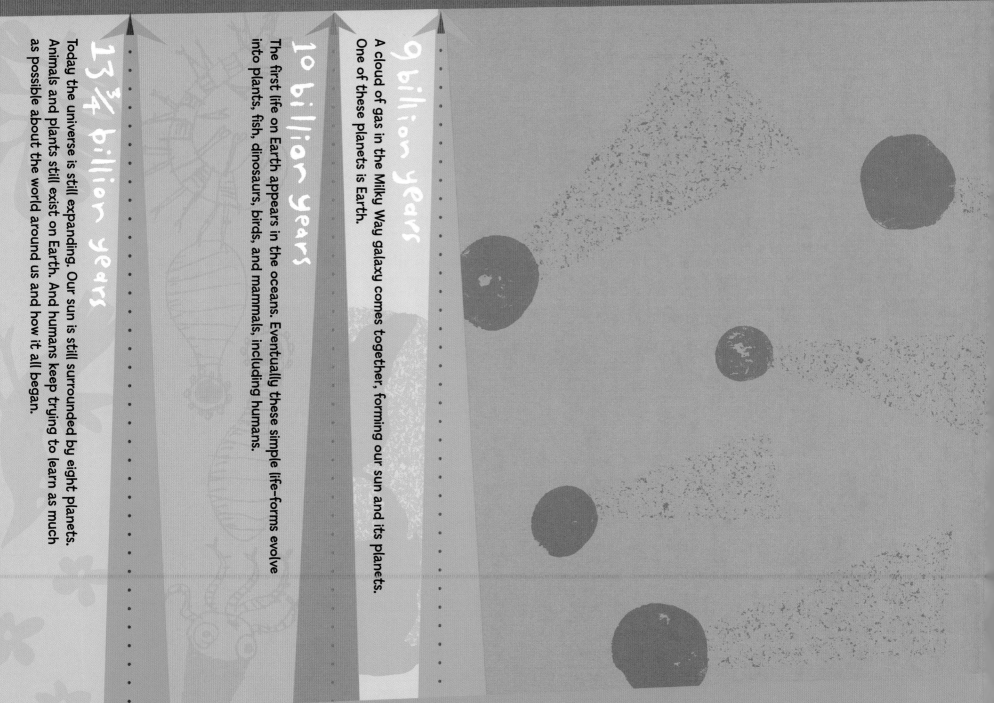

9 billion years

A cloud of gas in the Milky Way galaxy comes together, forming our sun and its planets. One of these planets is Earth.

10 billion years

The first life on Earth appears in the oceans. Eventually these simple life-forms evolve into plants, fish, dinosaurs, birds, and mammals, including humans.

13 3/4 billion years

Today the universe is still expanding. Our sun is still surrounded by eight planets. Animals and plants still exist on Earth. And humans keep trying to learn as much as possible about the world around us and how it all began.

Glossary

atom: A tiny particle that is made of even smaller particles called neutrons, electrons, and protons. There are over a hundred different kinds of atoms. Some are light, like helium, and some are heavier, like gold.

Big Bang: The initial explosion in which the universe was born.

carbon: A kind of atom. Carbon is very important for life to survive, as all plants, animals, and humans on Earth have carbon in them.

electron: One of the three particles that make up atoms. Electrons can also exist outside an atom—electricity, for example, is made when free electrons move through a material.

helium: A kind of very light atom, lighter than air but slightly heavier than hydrogen. Helium is a gas that is often used to fill up balloons so that they are light enough to rise up into the sky.

hydrogen: The very lightest atom possible. All by itself, hydrogen is usually a gas, but it is also a key ingredient of water.

minerals: Collections of atoms that are a part of Earth's crust. Sometimes they are made of just one kind of atom—like iron or gold. Sometimes they are made of different kinds of atoms bound together—like quartz, which is made of silicon and oxygen atoms.

neutron: One of the three particles that make up atoms.

particle: Any of the tiny, unseeable bits and blocks—such as electrons, protons, neutrons, and atoms—that come together to create all the larger things we see on Earth.

planet: Any large body that circles a star. In our solar system there are eight planets orbiting the sun: Mercury, Venus, Earth, Mars, Jupiter, Saturn, Uranus, and Neptune.

proton: One of the three particles that make up atoms.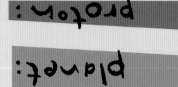

solar system: What we call our sun and all the planets that orbit it. There are other solar systems in the universe with planets circling other stars.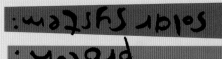

universe: Every single thing in existence—all the stars, all the planets, all the space, everything.